Copperfield

Charles Dickens

Abridged and adapted by Richard Paul

Illustrated by Carol Stutz

A PACEMAKER CLASSIC

Fearon/Janus/Quercus
Belmont, California

Simon & Schuster Education Group

Pacemaker Classics

The Adventures of Huckleberry Finn
The Adventures of Tom Sawyer
The Call of the Wild
A Christmas Carol
Crime and Punishment
David Copperfield
The Deerslayer
Dr. Jekyll and Mr. Hyde
Ethan Frome
Frankenstein
Great Expectations
Heart of Darkness
The Hunchback of Notre Dame
Jane Eyre
The Jungle Book
The Last of the Mohicans

The Mayor of Casterbridge
Moby Dick
The Moonstone
O Pioneers!
The Prince and the Pauper
The Red Badge of Courage
Robinson Crusoe
The Scarlet Letter
A Tale of Two Cities
The Three Musketeers
The Time Machine
Treasure Island
20,000 Leagues Under the Sea
Two Years Before the Mast
The War of the Worlds
Wuthering Heights

Library of Congress Catalog Card Number: 92–72580

ISBN 0–8224–9339–X

Printed in the United States of America

2. 10 9 8 7 6 5 4 3 2 1
MA

Contents

1 My Early Life

I was born on a Friday at twelve o'clock at night. I have been told that the clock began to strike, and I began to cry at the very same time.

My mother had been ill that afternoon. For six months she had also been low in spirits, ever since my father's death. As she sat by the fire, she saw a strange lady coming up the garden.

Instead of ringing the bell, the woman looked in through the window. She frowned. Then she waved to my mother, signaling that she was to open the door. It seemed that this woman was used to being obeyed. My mother went to let her in.

"Mrs. Copperfield?" asked the stranger.

"Yes," said my mother faintly.

"Miss Trotwood . . ." said the visitor. "You have heard of her, I dare say?"

My mother answered that she had.

Miss Betsey Trotwood was my father's aunt. She lived a long way off, however. She and my mother had never met.

"Now you see her," said Miss Betsey.

My mother bent her head and asked the lady to walk in.

"Well," said Miss Betsey as they sat down. "When do you expect the baby . . . "

"I am shaking," cried my mother. "I don't know what's the matter. I shall die, I am sure!"

"No, no, no," said Miss Betsey. "Have some tea."

Peggotty, the servant, was sent for. Peggotty was her last name. My father had always called her by that name because her first name was the same as my mother's.

"Peggotty!" cried Miss Betsey. "Tea for your mistress. She is not well. Hurry!"

She shut the parlor door and sat down as before. "I have no question about the baby. It shall be a girl," she declared.

"It might well be a boy," my mother put in.

"No, it shall be a girl. I intend to be her godmother. I will make it my business to see that she is well brought up. I ask that you call her Betsey Trotwood Copperfield."

My mother was too weak and upset to know what to say. Peggotty, coming in with tea and lighted candles, could see my mother's ill situation. Without delay, she took my mother up to her room. Then she sent Ham Peggotty, her nephew, to bring the doctor.

Mr. Chillip, the doctor, spent the evening with my mother, while Miss Betsey waited in the parlor. All night, sounds of feet and voices could be heard coming from my mother's room. Then, shortly after

midnight, a very red Doctor Chillip came down to the parlor. He spoke to my aunt.

"Well, I am happy to congratulate you."

"What upon?" said my aunt, sharply.

"All is over, and well over."

"How is she?" asked my aunt.

"Well. Quite as well as you would want for a young mother."

"And she? How is she?" asked my aunt.

The doctor tilted his head a little to one side, looking at my aunt like a friendly bird.

"The baby," said my aunt. "How is she?"

"Dear lady," returned the doctor. "I thought you knew! It's a boy."

My aunt never said another word. She took her bonnet by the strings, swung it at Chillip's head, put it on, and walked out. She never came back. That seemed to be our last of Miss Betsey Trotwood.

Upstairs, I lay in my basket in the land of dreams.

Such is the beginning of my story.

Looking back toward my infant life, I can remember well my mother and Clara Peggotty. I remember well the two sitting rooms in our house. One we used evenings, when Mother, Peggotty, and I would sit and talk at day's end. The other room, less comfortable, was used formally on Sundays. My mother read Bible stories to Peggotty and me in that room.

I remember, also, the churchyard. I see it out of the bedroom window. There is nothing half so green as the grass of that yard. There is nothing half so shady as its trees. There is nothing half so quiet as its tombstones. The sheep are often feeding there in the mornings as I wake from sleep.

Here is our seat in the church. It has a window nearby, out of which I can see our house in the distance. Though Peggotty looks around in church, she gets angry if I do. It is always she who reminds me to look straight ahead. Still, I can't help looking at our house. I see its bedroom windows standing open. I see the garden. I see the empty birdhouse and doghouse. I see fruit on the trees. Then a great wind rises, and the summer is over. Then we are playing in the winter's evening, dancing about the house. These things I remember.

One Sunday night, Peggotty and I were reading together in the sitting room. The bell in the garden rang. We went to the door, and there was Mother, looking very pretty. With her was a gentleman with beautiful black hair. He patted me on the head; but somehow, I didn't like him. I put his hand away as well as I could.

"Oh, Davy!" cried my mother.

"Dear boy!" said the gentleman. "Come. Let us be the best friends in the world."

The next Sunday the gentleman was with us in

church and walked home with us afterward. He came in, too, to look at a flower. My mother gave him the blossom. He promised that he would never, never part with it. I thought him to be quite a fool not to know that it would fall to pieces in a day or two.

I became used to seeing this gentleman with the black hair. However, I found that I liked him no better than at first. He even took me places. We rode horses together and went to a hotel by the sea. We walked together on the cliffs and looked at things through a telescope. I now knew him as Mr. Murdstone. My feelings toward him still had not changed.

One day, Peggotty came to me with an offer. "Master Davy, how would you like to spend two weeks with me at my brother's at Yarmouth? Would that not be a treat?"

"Is your brother a friendly man?" I asked.

"Oh, what a friendly man he is!" cried Peggotty. "Then there's also the sea and the boats and Ham to play with."

I answered that it would indeed be a treat. But what would my mother say?

"I'll ask her as soon as she comes home," said Peggotty.

My mother was not nearly so much surprised as I expected she would be. In fact, she agreed to it quickly. It was all arranged that night. I was beside myself with excitement.

However, I could not have suspected then how my life was about to change forever. It saddens me now to think of my eagerness to leave our happy home. I remember how my mother kissed me when I left. It was then that I cried. I was glad to see that my mother cried, too. When the horse and cart finally began to move, my mother called the driver to stop. She kissed me once more.

As we left Mother standing in the road, Mr. Murdstone joined her. He seemed to quarrel with her for being so moved. I looked back and wondered how it was any of his business.

The next two weeks I spent playing with Ham and little Emily. I believe I fell in love then with little Emily. Ham and Emily were cousins, the children of two of Mr. Peggotty's brothers who were no longer living. Mr. Peggotty was raising them.

After several pleasant days with my newly made friends, at last the day came for my return home. I was sad to leave Mr. Peggotty and Ham. However, the pain of leaving little Emily was almost more than I could bear.

Still, I was cheerful to be returning home. How well I remember the day. It was a cold, gray afternoon, with a dull sky. Upon reaching home, I opened the door and looked inside the house for

Mother. I saw only a strange servant.

"Why, Peggotty!" I said. "Isn't she home?"

"Yes, yes, Master Davy," said Peggotty. "She's home. Wait a bit, and I'll . . . I'll tell you something."

She took me by the hand and shut the door.

"Peggotty," I cried. "What's the matter?"

"I should have told you before. What do you think? You have got a pa!" Very quickly I turned white and felt shaky.

We then went straight to our best sitting room. Peggotty left me. On one side of the fire sat my mother. On the other side sat Mr. Murdstone. My mother rose.

"Now, Clara," said Mr. Murdstone, "Control yourself. Davy boy, how do you do?"

I gave him my hand. I kissed my mother. I could not look at her. I could not look at him. Then, as soon as I could, I left for my bedroom. But my bedroom had been changed, and I was now to sleep a long way away from my mother.

Shortly I found that it was not only my room that had changed. My whole life was changing. No longer did my mother and Peggotty and I sit together. No longer did we read together in the evenings. In fact, as the days passed, I hardly saw the two of them. I had come under the control of Mr. Murdstone and his sister, Jane, who had come to live with us. Miss Murdstone took over all of the things that my mother had done before. Surely, Mother and I were like visitors in our own home.

Then one day Mr. Murdstone and I had a quarrel. He felt that I had not tried to learn my lessons well. I told him that I could not learn with him standing over me. Soon we were alone in my bedroom, and he was giving me a beating. Do not ask why, but for some dreadful reason I bit the hand that was beating me.

After that I was jailed in my room for five days straight. I cannot tell you how much longer than that those days seemed to last. I even came to miss hearing the sound of my own voice.

Then Miss Murdstone came to me. She told me that I was going away to school. It seemed that I was a wicked fellow. Going away to school was to improve me.

When it was the hour that I should leave, Mother told me, "You are going for your own good, Davy. When you come home, you will be a better boy."

"Clara!" warned Miss Murdstone.

"Yes, my dear Jane," answered my mother. "God bless you, my Davy."

Miss Murdstone was good enough to see me out to the cart. On the way she said she hoped that I would be a better boy. Then I got into the cart, and the lazy horse walked off with it.

2 Away at School

We might have gone about half a mile when the driver stopped short. To my surprise, I saw Peggotty climb into the cart. She took me in both her arms and hugged me until it hurt. She didn't speak a single word. Then she gave me some paper bags of cakes and some money. After a final hug, she got down from the cart and ran away.

The driver looked at me as if to ask if she were coming back. I shook my head and said I thought not. "Then come on," said the driver to the lazy horse.

I asked the driver (whose name was Mr. Barkis) if he was going all the way.

"All the way where?"

"To London," I said.

"Why, that horse would be deader than pork before we got half over the ground!"

"Are you only going to Yarmouth, then?" I asked.

"That's about it," said the driver. "You'll take a coach to London."

I slept most of the way to Yarmouth. I guess I was tired from the strain of leaving home. First, though, I offered Mr. Barkis one of Peggotty's cakes, which he

accepted. He ate it in one gulp, exactly like an elephant.

"Did she make them now?"

"Do you mean Peggotty, sir?"

"Ah!" said Mr. Barkis. "Her."

"Yes. She does all our cooking."

"When you write to her, would you say that Barkis was willing?" he asked.

"That Barkis was willing," I repeated. "Is that all?"

"Yes. Barkis is willing."

I promised to write the message to Peggotty. Being only eight years old, I really didn't know what it meant.

From Yarmouth, where I didn't get to see little Emily, I took the coach to London. We started at three o'clock in the afternoon. We were due in London about eight the next morning.

It was summer weather, and the evening was very pleasant. Whenever we passed through a village, I pictured to myself what the insides of the houses were like. When I saw boys playing, I wondered if their fathers were alive and if they were happy at home. Between villages, I wondered about London and the new school. I had heard in Yarmouth that a boy's ribs had been broken at the school. They had been broken during a whipping.

When we arrived in London, nobody was there to claim the dusty youngster from Blunderstone. Once the horses were taken out and the coach put away, I felt quite alone.

By and by, a man in a black suit came up to me. "You're the new boy?" he asked.

"Yes, sir," I said. (I supposed I was. I didn't know.)

"Come with me. I'll take you to Salem House. It's about six miles away."

The school was a square brick building with wings. Mr. Mell, the teacher, met me right away. Everything was so very quiet that I said to him I supposed the boys were out. He seemed surprised that I didn't know that it was holiday time. All the boys were at home with their families. The owner, Mr. Creakle, was down by the sea with his wife. I learned then that I had been sent at holiday time as punishment. I was to wear a sign that read: Take care of him. He bites.

You cannot imagine the pain that sign caused me. I had to wear it all day, every day. My days with Mr. Mell lasted until seven or eight in the evening. Then when I walked about, I was watched over by the man who had brought me from London.

I had led this life for about a month when Mr. Creakle returned. One day I was fetched to appear before him.

"So!" said Mr. Creakle. "You are the young gentleman whose teeth are to be filed. What's the report on this boy?"

Mr. Creakle was told there was nothing against me yet. I thought he was disappointed. He warned me, anyway, to stay out of trouble. Then he pinched my ear and told me to get out of his room. His parting words were, "I am a Tartar."

I had heard that Mr. Creakle had good reason to call himself a Tartar. He was the meanest of masters. He liked to charge in among the boys and slash away with his cane. His favorite whipping boy was Tommy Traddles, who was just about my age. Tommy and I became good friends.

School began for real the next day. Mr. Creakle spoke to us.

"Now, boys, this is a new semester. Take care of how you act. Come fresh to the lessons, I tell you, for I will be fresh for your punishments. It will be of no use to rub your wounds. You won't rub out the marks that I shall give you. Now get to work, every boy."

There was one good thing about Mr. Creakle's punishments. He often found that my sign was in his way when he used his cane on me from behind. For this reason, the sign was soon taken off, and I saw it no more.

My life at Salem House was made easier by the boy I roomed with—James Steerforth. Steerforth was, at about fifteen, one of the oldest boys. He protected me as best he could and showed me how to get along at school. He made sure the other boys didn't bother me.

Still, he did get kindly Mr. Mell fired by insulting him in front of Mr. Creakle. Steerforth had learned from me that Mr. Mell's mother was in the poorhouse. When Mr. Creakle heard that from Steerforth, he fired the teacher on the spot. Then he made a speech in which he thanked Steerforth. I felt terrible. Poor Tommy Traddles got the cane for being in tears over Mr. Mell's firing.

The half year at Salem House is a wild mix of memories for me. I remember the passing summer and the changing seasons. I remember cold mornings when we were rung out of bed. I remember the cold, cold smell of the dark nights when we were rung into bed. I remember the schoolroom, dimly lighted and carelessly warmed. I remember dog-eared books, cracked slates, tear-blotted pages of notes, cane beatings, hair cuttings, rainy Sundays, and a dirty air of ink around everything.

Finally, the holidays came. I was scheduled to go home, but I feared terribly that something would keep me from leaving. At last, I woke up one morning when the ground outside the window was not the playground of Salem House. The sound in my ears was not the sound of Mr. Creakle giving it to Traddles. I was aboard the Yarmouth mail carrier.

And the sound was the coach driver yelling "get along" to the horses.

I arrived home at a good time. Mr. and Miss Murdstone had gone out visiting and would not return before evening. I had never hoped for such luck. Alone with my mother and Peggotty, I felt as if the old days had come back.

We dined together by the fire. Then we sat around the fire and talked. I told them what a hard master Mr. Creakle was, and they pitied me. I crept close to my mother's side and sat with my arms around her waist. When we had had our tea, I read to Peggotty from one of our favorite books. Then we talked more about Salem House, and I talked about Steerforth, who was my favorite subject. We were very happy. That evening will never pass from my memory.

The Murdstones came home about ten o'clock that evening. They brought into the house a cold blast of air that blew away the old warm feeling like a feather. I hurried up to my bedroom before they saw me. They did not like late hours for young people.

The next morning I greeted Mr. Murdstone. "I beg your pardon, sir. I am very sorry for what I did, and I hope you will forgive me."

"I am glad to hear you are sorry, David," he replied.

"How do you do, ma'am?" I said to Miss Murdstone.

"Ah, dear me!" said Miss Murdstone. "How long are the holidays?"

"A month, ma'am."

"Oh!" said Miss Murdstone. "Then here's one day off." She kept a calendar of the holidays. Every morning she checked off a day in the same way.

During the whole month, I was not allowed in my room except to sleep. Because she was a servant, I was also no longer allowed to sit or to read or to eat with Peggotty. Instead, I had my meals in silence. At the table I began to feel that there was a knife and fork too many—mine.

So the holidays lagged away. Then the morning came when Miss Murdstone announced, "Here's the last day off."

I was not sorry to go. I kissed my mother goodbye—and was sorry then. But I was not sorry to go away.

The last voice I heard was Miss Murdstone's. "Clara," she warned, as my mother started to bid me farewell. I looked back only once. My mother stood alone in the cold, still weather. She had a new life now.

3   I Go to Work

Two months after my return to Salem House, I was called into the sitting room. A smelly fog hung about the place. The raw cold made us blow on our fingers and tap our feet to keep warm. I have reason to remember that day above all others. It was my tenth birthday. I thought I had gotten some food from Peggotty.

I was announced: "David Copperfield to see Mrs. Creakle."

"David Copperfield," said Mrs. Creakle. "I have something to tell you, my child."

Mr. Creakle shook his head without looking at me.

"I have to tell you that I hear this morning that your mama is very ill," said Mrs. Creakle.

A mist rose between us.

"She is dangerously ill," she added.

I knew all now.

"She is dead," she explained.

There was no need to tell me so. I had already begun crying.

Mrs. Creakle was very kind to me. She kept me there all day. I cried myself to sleep and woke up and cried again. When I could cry no more, I began to think. Then my grief became a dull pain for which there was no relief.

I left Salem House for home the next afternoon. I hardly thought then that I would never return.

When my coach reached home, I jumped out the back as quickly as possible. I was in Peggotty's arms before I got to the door. She took me into the house. Mr. Murdstone took no notice of me but sat by the fire, weeping quietly.

Miss Murdstone was busy at her desk. Her only words to me were "Have you brought your shirts home?"

"Yes, ma'am. I have brought all my clothes home," I answered.

My mother was buried beside my father in the churchyard, where I had so often heard the birds sing on summer mornings. That day there was a hush. The day was different from every other day. Even the light was not of the same color. It was of a sadder color.

When it was over and the earth was filled in, we turned to go away. Before us stood our house. The house remained pretty and unchanged. It reminded me only of my mother. All my sorrow had been nothing to the sorrow it called forth.

After the funeral, Miss Murdstone's first act of business was to give Peggotty a month's notice. As much as Peggotty would have disliked staying, I believe she would have done so for my sake. The matter was settled for her, however.

As for me or my future, not a word was said, nor a step taken. I think they would have been happy to get rid of me with a month's notice, too.

I was soon allowed to go with Peggotty to Yarmouth for a visit. While I was there, Peggotty and Mr. Barkis were married. (He had been willing for a long time.) When I returned home, it was just as it had been before. My days were spent alone reading or dreaming. I was not beaten or starved, but day after day, week after week, month after month, I was coldly neglected.

Oh, what I would have given to be sent away to a school! No such hope came to me. The Murdstones disliked me, and they left me alone.

One morning after breakfast I had put my chair away and was going out of the room. Mr. Murdstone called me back.

"I believe, David, that it would not help you to be kept at school," he said. "What is ahead of you is a fight with the world. The sooner you begin it, the better."

He went on to say that I was to go to work at his place of business in London. The work would provide for my eating and drinking and pocket money. He would pay for my room.

I felt they just wanted to get rid of me—though I

didn't have long to think about it. I was to leave the next morning.

Mr. Murdstone's partner was Mr. Grinby. Their business was at the waterfront, in a crazy old house at the bottom of a narrow street. The place was overrun with rats. Its rooms were gray from the dirt and smoke of a hundred years.

Murdstone and Grinby did business with many kinds of people, though selling wine to ships was their main business. My job was to wash empty bottles and paste labels on full ones. I hated the work. My hopes of growing up to be an important man were over. I longed for Steerforth, Traddles, and the rest of the boys at Salem House. Most days my tears mixed with the water in which I washed the bottles.

My room was in the rundown house of the Micawber family. Mr. Micawber knew Mr. Murdstone, which accounted for this arrangement. There was also a Mrs. Micawber and four small children.

The Micawbers were very poor. I heard about it from Mrs. Micawber when she first showed me my room. "I never thought," she said, "that I would need to take a boarder. But being in hard times, all thoughts of my own feelings must give way."

I said, "Yes, ma'am."

"He owes a lot of people," she said. "You can't get blood from a stone. Neither can they get money from Mr. Micawber at this time."

Poor Mrs. Micawber. The creditors came at all hours, and some of them were quite mean. One dirty-faced man came at seven o'clock in the morning. He called up the stairs to Mr. Micawber: "Come, pay us, will you. Don't hide, you know. Just pay us."

One evening, Mrs. Micawber came crying to me. "Master Copperfield," she said, "Mr. Micawber is about at the end. There is nothing to eat in the house."

"Dear me!" I said, in great sorrow.

I offered the loan of the three shillings I had in my pocket. Mrs. Micawber wouldn't take it. Instead, she begged me to sell her plates and other things for food money. This I did, a few at a time, for several weeks.

The time came, however, when there was nothing left to sell. One morning Mr. Micawber was arrested and carried over to the King's Bench Prison. Mrs. Micawber and the children moved into the prison as well. I found a little room near the prison.

All this time, I had been working at Murdstone and Grinby's. I had never made a single friend. I led a private life, but I led it in a self-reliant manner. Often I would have breakfast with the Micawbers in their jail cell. I forget at what hour the jail gates were opened. I do know, though, that I was often up at six o'clock. My favorite place to wait before breakfast was Old London Bridge. I would sit and watch the people going by and wonder what might happen to me next.

I visited the Micawbers every evening. Then, when Mr. Micawber's sentence was up, he and his wife decided to move their family to Plymouth. There they hoped to start a new life.

I remember their parting words: "Master Copperfield, God bless you," said Mrs. Micawber. "I can never forget you, and I never would if I could."

Mr. Micawber said, "Farewell Copperfield. I hope my life has been a warning to you. When something turns up for me, I shall be very happy if it should be in my power to help you."

Mrs. Micawber gave me just such a kiss as she might have given her own boy. I guess she saw what a little fellow I really was. I stood in the middle of the road and watched their coach move away. Then I went to begin my weary day at Murdstone and Grinby's.

However, I did not intend to pass many more weary days there. No, I had made up my mind to run away. I remembered that old story about my birth. It came to me that I should go to the only relative I had in the world. I would go to my aunt, Miss Betsey.

I wrote a letter to Peggotty asking where Miss Betsey lived. Peggotty answered that she was

somewhere near Dover. By the end of the week, I was preparing for my journey. My baggage would travel by coach, and I would travel by foot. Yet before I had even left the city, my baggage and money were stolen. I traveled to Miss Betsey's with only the clothes on my back.

Six days later, I arrived at Dover. It took some doing, but at last I was able to find a man who knew where my aunt lived. He directed me to a very neat little cottage with a garden full of flowers.

A lady wearing a pair of gardening gloves came out of the house. I approached her with great fear. My shoes were broken; my hat, crushed and bent; and my shirt and pants, torn and stained. My hair had not known a comb since I left London.

"Go away!" said Miss Betsey. "Go along! No boys here!"

"If you please, ma'am," I began.

She started off, then looked up.

"If you please, Aunt."

"What?" said Miss Betsey, in a tone of surprise.

"If you please, Aunt, I am your nephew."

"Oh, Lord!" said my aunt. And she sat flat down in the garden path.

4 My Life Gets Better

"I am David Copperfield, of Blunderstone. You came on the night when I was born and saw my dear mama. I have not been very happy since she died. I have been slighted and taught nothing. I have been left to fend for myself and put to work not fit for me. It made me run away to you."

I sobbed out these words to Miss Betsey.

"Mercy on us," said my aunt. "Your sister, Betsey Trotwood, never would have run away." My aunt shook her head, certain that the girl who had never been born would not have behaved as I had.

Still, I was fed and bathed and taken up to a pleasant room to sleep. This room was at the top of the house and looked out over the sea. I remember how I sat looking at the moonlight on the water as if I could read my fortune in it. I prayed that I might never again be homeless. I prayed that I might never forget the homeless. I seemed to float, then, away into the world of dreams.

On going down in the morning, I found my aunt in deep thought. I knew that she was thinking about me. I wondered what her intentions were.

Aunt Betsey let me know after breakfast. "I have

written to him," she told me.

"To?"

"To your stepfather," she said.

"Does he know where I am?" I asked, worried.

"I have told him," said my aunt, with a nod.

"Shall I . . . be . . . given up to him?"

"I don't know," said my aunt. "We shall see." My spirits sank low from these words.

Several days later, Mr. and Miss Murdstone arrived. Miss Murdstone made the mistake of riding her donkey over Miss Betsey's lawn. Miss Betsey found nothing more troublesome than donkeys on her lawn. It seemed to set her against the Murdstones. Once everyone had settled in, Mr. Murdstone got right to the point.

"I am here to take David back," he said. "I will do with him as I think proper and deal with him as I think right. I am here for the first and the last time. Is he ready to go? If you tell me he is not, my doors are shut against him forever. I then will take it for granted that yours are open to him."

"What does the boy say?" asked my aunt. "Are you ready to go, David?"

I begged her not to let me go. I said that neither Mr. nor Miss Murdstone had ever liked me. They had never been kind to me. They had made my mother unhappy about me. I begged my aunt to protect me for my father's sake. And so she did.

"You can go when you like," she told Mr. Murdstone. "I'll take my chances with the boy." Then she turned to Miss Murdstone. "You ride a donkey over my lawn again, and as sure as you have a head upon your shoulders, I'll knock your hat off." Thus, I began a new life. I even had a new name. My aunt called me Trotwood Copperfield.

My aunt took kindly to me. In the course of a few weeks, she shortened my new name to Trot.

One evening she said, "Trot, we must not forget your education. Would you like to go to school at Canterbury?"

I answered that I would like it very much.

"Good. We shall go tomorrow."

I was greatly pleased by these orders.

The next day my aunt drove to a very old house in Canterbury. The owner was Mr. Wickfield, a friend of hers. Mr. Wickfield helped my aunt find a good school for me. He also offered to let me stay at his house while I was in school. The only bad thing about this arrangement was Uriah Heep.

Uriah Heep was a boy of fifteen who worked for Mr. Wickfield. He frightened me somewhat. He had a very pale face, but that wasn't the worst of it. Far worse were his eyes. They looked like two red suns. Whenever I looked toward those suns, they were either just rising or just setting.

On the other hand, Agnes Wickfield was a joy. She

was Mr. Wickfield's daughter and a girl of my own age. Her peaceful brightness made me think of a stained glass window in a church.

The school was very good. It was as different from Mr. Creakle's as good is from evil. Doctor Strong, the master, was loved by every boy. He was the kindest of men, with a simple faith. He was known to give the clothes off his back to beggars. Everything about him brought out the honor and good faith of the boys.

My school days! The silent gliding on of my life. The unseen progress from childhood to youth. I can remember . . . my place in the church, where we all went together every Sunday morning. The smell of earth, the feeling of the world being shut out, the sound of the organ. These are things that take me back to those days.

I am not the last boy in my class. I have risen, in a few months, over several others. But the first boy seems to me to be so far off that I'll never pass him. Agnes says, "You can pass him." But I say "no." He is not my friend and protector, as Steerforth was. Still, I hold him in respect. Mostly I wonder what he'll be when he leaves Doctor Strong's.

When he does leave, I am the head boy. I look down upon the line of boys below me. I see, too, the boy I was not so long ago. That little fellow seems to be no part of me, now that I am 17. I remember him as something left behind on the road of life.

Where is the little girl I saw on that first day at Mr. Wickfield's? Gone also. Now a mature young woman moves about in her stead: Agnes, my sweet sister, my friend. She is more like an angel than is anyone who comes near her.

There is one more thing to tell about my youth. I fell in love with a 30-year-old woman. When she married a farmer, I was very sad but just for a week or two. It was only a mark in my journey to age 17.

5 I Become a Man

I don't know whether I was glad or sorry when my school days came to an end. I was very happy at school. I was fond of Doctor Strong. I was a success in that little world. For these reasons, I was sorry to go. But for other reasons, I was glad.

I had misty ideas of being a young man on my own. I dreamed of wonderful things to be seen and done. I longed to do some good in the world. My aunt and I had many talks about what work I should do. But I had no particular liking for anything. My desire was to do something that wouldn't cost my aunt too much money.

"Trot, I tell you what," said my aunt one morning. "It seems to me that a little change may be helpful to you. Suppose you were to go down into the old part of the country again. You could see Peggotty."

"Of all the things in the world, Aunt, I should like it best."

"Well," said my aunt, "that's lucky. I should like it, too."

Shortly thereafter I was given a large sum of money and sent upon my journey. At parting, my aunt gave me a good many kisses. She told me to take three weeks or a month to look about and think a little.

I stopped in Canterbury first. Agnes was very glad to see me. We talked and joked with one another for a time, as old friends do. But then Agnes suddenly spoke in a different tone.

"Trotwood, there is something that I want to ask you. Have you noticed a change in Papa?"

I had seen it and wondered if she had, too.

"Yes," I said. "I think he does himself no good by his habit of drinking. I think I have seen that habit get worse since I first came here."

"You are right," said Agnes.

"His hand shakes, his speech is not plain, and his eyes look wild," I said. "When he is least like himself, he is most certain to be wanted on some business."

"By Uriah Heep," said Agnes.

Just then Agnes's father came into the room. Agnes and I were never able to finish our talk. I could only stay for a brief time before going on to London. I heard no more about Uriah Heep from Agnes.

I got a joyous surprise at my hotel in London. As I was eating dinner, I saw a handsome young man come in. I could hardly believe my eyes. It was my roommate from Salem House.

"Steerforth, won't you say hello!" I cried.

"My God!" he shouted. "It's little Copperfield!"

"My dear Steerforth, I am overjoyed to see you!" I grabbed both his hands and could not let them go.

"And I am rejoiced to see you, too!" he said. "What brings you here?"

I told him about my aunt and about finishing school in Canterbury. "How is it that you are here, Steerforth?" I asked.

He answered that he was going to college at Oxford. He was now on his way to visit his mother. He insisted that I go with him so that we might have plenty of time to talk. I was happy to do so.

Steerforth's mother lived in an old brick house on the top of a hill. It was a very quiet and orderly house. From its windows all of London could be seen. Mrs. Steerforth was an elderly lady. She had a pleasant face, and she carried herself proudly.

"My dear James," she said as she greeted us. It was clear that she was very fond of her son. She gave me a formal welcome.

A week passed in a most delightful way. Steerforth's servant, a man named Littimer, gave us the best of care. He brought us horses, and Steerforth gave me lessons in riding. He brought us foils, and Steerforth gave me lessons in fencing. He brought gloves, and I began to improve in boxing. I built up a true liking for the servant and a new admiration for his master.

By and by Steerforth made up his mind to go with

me into the country. We took a coach to Yarmouth, where we stayed the night at an inn. Then we agreed that I would go alone to the Peggottys. Steerforth would come along later, after I had been "cried over for a few hours."

I was cried over. "My darling boy!" cried Peggotty when she saw who I was. It must have been seven years since we had seen each other. At first, she didn't know me. But when I called her name, she recognized my voice. Then we hugged and laughed and cried all at the same time. She took me up to see Mr. Barkis, who was now an invalid and he spent most of his time in bed.

It was not long before Steerforth came. Because of his easy manner, he and Peggotty became friends within minutes. We stayed for dinner, and afterward we visited Mr. Barkis in his room and had a merry time.

At eight o'clock we set off for Mr. Peggotty's houseboat. We walked over the dark winter sands toward the old boat. I was anxious to see my dear friends Emily and Ham and Mr. Peggotty again. Around us the wind was sighing mournfully.

"This is a wild kind of place, Steerforth, is it not?"

"It sure is in the dark," he said. "And the sea roars as if it were hungry for us."

We found Mr. Peggotty, little Emily, and Ham in a joyous state. The reason for their merry clapping

and laughing was soon made known to us. Little Emily and Ham had just told Mr. Peggotty that they were going to be married. Soon we were all shaking hands with one another. We were telling one another how glad we were to meet again, all talking at once. I thought I had never seen Ham grin as widely as he was grinning then. Little Emily was charming.

We sat and talked for quite a while. Once I asked little Emily if she remembered how I used to be in love with her. We both laughed, and her face grew red. She seemed to spend most of the evening with her eyes fixed on Steerforth. Finally, we parted about midnight. I saw the sweet blue eyes of little Emily peeping after us from behind Ham. I heard her soft voice calling to us to be careful how we went.

Steerforth and I stayed in Yarmouth for more than two full weeks. We were together a lot of that time. Yet very often we were apart. I was interested in going to Blunderstone to see again the places of my childhood. Steerforth had no desire to go there with me. Then, too, I did not like to stay out late at night. Steerforth was a person who enjoyed doing so. He spent many nights at sea, coming back when the morning tide was at flood level. I never asked him what he did when he was not with me.

One dark evening, I found Steerforth alone in Mr. Peggotty's house. He was sitting and staring at the fire. I had come back from my last visit to

Blunderstone. He was so deep in thought that he did not hear me come in. I was standing quite close to him before he jumped at seeing me.

"You come upon me like a ghost!" he shouted. After an apology from me, he cooled down. Then he said words such as I had never heard from him.

"David, I wish I'd had a father these last 20 years."

"My dear Steerforth, what is the matter?"

"I wish with all of my soul that I had been better guided!" he cried. "I wish with all of my soul that I could direct myself better!"

This made very little sense to me. A night later, I was just as puzzled by an outburst from little Emily. We were sitting with her and Peggotty and Ham. Ham had said how much he loved her.

"Oh, Ham," she said, weeping. "I am not so good a girl as I ought to be. It might have been better for you if you had become fond of someone else."

The next morning Steerforth and I left by coach. Peggotty and all her family were full of sorrow at our going. I, too, was sad about it. Still, when we were on our way, my spirits picked up. I showed Steerforth a letter that my aunt had sent me. She had found a job for me as clerk in a law office if I wanted it. Steerforth thought it would be a dull job. I wasn't sure.

At our journey's end, my aunt came to London to meet me. Steerforth went home, and I went to

Lincoln's Inn Fields, where my aunt was staying. Miss Betsey pressed me to take the job she had found. She told me it would cost her a thousand pounds to get me into the law firm. Hearing that, I objected strongly. Then she said a most wonderful thing.

"Trot, my child, I have one object in life. That is to make you a good and a happy man."

With that, I agreed to her plan. I quickly became a clerk in the firm of Spenlow and Jorkins. I began a month's trial the next day.

My aunt also found a place for me to live in London. It was a set of rooms on Buckingham Street, with a view of the river. I had a sitting room, a bedroom, and a kitchen. The furniture was a little old but quite good enough for me. Best of all, the rent was not too high. I was delighted with the place. I was ready to begin my life as a young gentlemen.

6 Dora and Emily

My work at Spenlow and Jorkins went well. I am happy to say that Mr. Spenlow took a liking to me rather quickly. His wife was dead, and his only daughter was away at school in Paris. When she came home, he said, he hoped to have the pleasure of entertaining me at his home.

Mr. Spenlow was as good as his word. He soon asked me to come down to Norwood on the next Saturday. He would be happy, he said, if I would stay until Monday. Of course, I said I would.

There was a lovely garden around Mr. Spenlow's house. Around the garden was a beautiful lawn. Groups of trees, flowers, and bushes grew along its walks. The house was cheerfully lighted. I entered it through a hall where there were all sorts of hats, caps, coats, gloves, whips, and walking sticks.

"Mr. Copperfield," said Mr. Spenlow, as he motioned toward his daughter. "My daughter Dora and my daughter's friend."

It was over in a moment. In an instant I was swallowed up in love. I was gone before I had sense enough to say a word to her.

Dora Spenlow's friend was none other than Miss

Murdstone. I later learned that she had been hired to watch over Dora. At the time, I hardly noticed her. I had thoughts only for Dora Spenlow. What a lovely form she had. What a lovely face. What a graceful manner.

I sat next to Dora at dinner. I don't remember who was there besides Dora. I haven't the slightest idea what we had for dinner. Dora had a delightful little voice and a joyous little laugh. Everything else I failed to notice.

The next day, Dora and I walked about in the garden. We looked at the flowers and played with her dog, Jip. We laughed, and we talked. It was an enjoyable time.

Before I left Norwood, I had a few moments alone with Miss Murdstone. She asked if we could keep our past a secret. I said I thought that she and Mr. Murdstone had used me cruelly. I added that they had treated my mother badly. However, I did agree that nothing would be gained by making our past known. Miss Murdstone touched the back of my hand with her cold fingers and walked away.

I really did not care much one way or the other about Miss Murdstone. She was simply a part of my youth that could not be done over.

My thoughts now were only with Dora Spenlow. I lived in a dream about her. I bought new clothes that I did not need because I thought they would please

her. Every day I walked miles upon miles, in hopes of seeing her. Sometimes I saw her in a passing carriage. Now and then I would meet her and Miss Murdstone and walk with them a little way. I was always looking out for another invitation to Mr. Spenlow's house. I was always being disappointed, for I got none.

One day, I met my old school friend Tommy Traddles. He invited me to visit him, which I did as soon as possible. He was renting some rooms in a very poor section of Camden Town. When I had found it, his place reminded me of the days when I lived with the Micawbers. You can guess my surprise when I learned that Mr. and Mrs. Micawber owned this house. Mr. Micawber was still waiting for "something to turn up." After leaving school Tommy Traddles had copied law rulings for a living. This had led him to the study of law. He was now working, as was I, in a law office. He also let me know that he was going to be married.

About this time, also, I got a letter from Peggotty. I learned that Mr. Barkis was very, very ill. Naturally, I went to Yarmouth at once. Mr. Spenlow was quite good about letting me off for a few days. When I asked for time off, I also asked about Miss Spenlow. She was very well, he told me, unaware of my feelings for her.

When I got to Peggotty's house, her brother was

there. So, too, were Ham and little Emily. We spoke in whispers, listening for sounds from the room above. They told me that Mr. Barkis was dying. Mr. Peggotty informed us that people along the coast could not die except at high tide.

By and by we went up to Mr. Barkis's room and watched him for a long time—for hours. He finally opened his eyes.

Mr. Peggotty whispered in my ear, "They are both going out fast."

"Barkis, my dear!" said Peggotty. "Look! Here is Master Davy."

I was just about to ask him if he knew me when he smiled and said, "Barkis is willing!" And, it being low water, he then went out with the tide.

Mr. Barkis was buried in the same churchyard as my mother and father. Only Peggotty, Mr. Peggotty, and I attended the funeral. That evening we spent comforting Peggotty in Mr. Peggotty's houseboat.

Later Ham came in crying. He had received terrible news. In his hand was a letter from little Emily. They were not going to be married. She had run away with someone else. Her letter read, in part:

> I will never come back unless he brings me back as a lady. Oh, how my heart is torn. I am too evil to write about myself. Love some girl who is

worthy of you. Tell my uncle that
I have never loved him half so dearly
as now.

"Who is it she has run away with?" I asked.

"Master Davy, it ain't your fault," said Ham, in a broken voice. "His name is Steerforth, and he is a damned villain!"

I could think of nothing to do at that moment. I wanted only to drop to my knees and beg forgiveness for the pain my friend had caused. I joined the others in shedding tears for our little lost Emily.

7 I Marry

My love for Dora had endured these latest painful turns of events. In fact, I now loved Dora more deeply than ever. I was joyous, then, when Mr. Spenlow told me about Dora's birthday. He said he would be delighted if I would come down and join them for a little picnic on her day. Of course I would.

It was a fine picnic, but I was jealous of every man who talked with Dora. I made up my mind that day to ask her to marry me. If she would not, I thought it would kill me.

Three days later, I asked Dora to marry me. She said yes! Oh, blessed day, she said yes! The joy I felt knew no limit. We decided to keep our engagement secret for a time.

Of course, I wrote to dear Agnes Wickfield as soon as Dora and I had become engaged. I wanted her to know of my deep love for Dora. As I was writing, I remembered Agnes's clear, calm eyes and her gentle face. A peaceful feeling came over me.

I said nothing of Steerforth. I only told her that there had been sorrow at Yarmouth because of Emily's departure.

To this letter I got a swift response. As I read

Agnes' letter, I seemed to hear her friendly voice speaking to me. I learned from her that Uriah Heep had become a full partner in her father's firm. Uriah Heep seemed to be gaining more and more control over her father.

A few days later, I went to visit Dora. I had been worrying about the lack of money. (My aunt had fallen on hard times and was no longer able to add to my small earnings.) This was the one thing most on my mind. Without thinking, I asked Dora if she could love a beggar. It frightened her.

"How can you ask me anything so foolish?" she said. Then she began to cry.

I told her again how deeply I loved her. I told her, though, that it would help our coming marriage if she would learn how to cook. I also mentioned keeping house and taking care of money. With that, she almost fainted. It was quite clear that my pretty Dora was not ready for such everyday duties.

The next Saturday when I went to the office, I was surprised to see everyone standing about. Nobody was doing anything. One of the clerks, old Tiffey, was the first to notice me.

"This is an awful day, Mr. Copperfield," he said.

"What is it? What's the matter?" I asked.

"Don't you know?" cried Tiffey. All the rest of them gathered round me.

"No!" I said, looking from face to face.

"Mr. Spenlow," said Tiffey.

"What about him?"

"Dead!"

"Dead?" I asked.

"He was driving to the office by himself. When his carriage arrived, it was empty. Three men immediately went out along the road to look for him. They found his body a mile away."

Mr. Spenlow's death was a loss for me. You can imagine what a terrible shock it was for Dora. A second shock followed shortly. He had left no will to provide for Dora. Rather, it was discovered that Mr. Spenlow had lived beyond his means. Dora was left with very little money. It was clear to me, in my twenty-first year, that I should marry Dora Spenlow as soon as possible.

We waited a decent time after the funeral. During that time, Dora lived with two of her aunts. I began writing for magazines and earned quite a bit of money. I was well-off by the time we were married.

On our wedding day I lapsed into a dream world the moment I reached the church door. Only as we drove away together did I finally wake from the dream. Still, it was hard to believe that standing beside me was my dear, dear little wife, whom I loved so well!

8 Joys and Sorrows

It was strange to sit down in my own small house with Dora. It was hard to believe that I no longer had to go out to see her. I no longer had to write to her. We had no one to please but each other.

I doubt that two young birds could have known less about keeping house. We had a servant, of course. Her name was Mary Anne Paragon. She was not a good cook. In fact, she was not good at anything. She was the cause of our first little quarrel.

I said one day to Dora, "My dear wife, do you think Mary Anne has any idea of time?"

"Why, Davy?" asked Dora.

"Because it's five o'clock, and we were to have dined at four."

My wife came and sat upon my knee.

I continued, "Don't you think, my dear, that it would be good for you to talk to Mary Anne?"

"Oh, no, please! I couldn't, Davy!" said Dora.

"Why not?" I gently asked.

"Because I am such a little goose," said Dora. "She knows I am."

Again, I urged her to talk to Mary Anne about her

work habits. "It is not pleasant to have to go without one's dinner," I said.

With that, Dora began to cry. I had wounded her soft little heart. Just then I had to hurry away for an appointment. I was kept out late, and I felt bad all evening. It was two hours past midnight when I got home. I found my aunt sitting up for me. (Her house was just across the garden.)

"Is anything the matter, Aunt?" I said, alarmed.

"Nothing, Trot," she answered. "Sit down. Sit down. Little blossom has been out of spirits. I have been keeping her company, that's all."

I said that I had tried to speak to her tenderly about our home.

"I know," said my aunt. "But little blossom is a very tender little blossom, and the wind must be gentle with her."

With this my aunt tied a scarf around her head, and I walked her home.

It is painful to remember all of the problems we had. We finally got rid of Mary Anne. Then we hired Mrs. Kidgerbury, who made a point of falling up and down the kitchen stairs. We got rid of her and several more after her.

Everybody we had anything to do with seemed to cheat Dora and me. When we appeared in a shop, it was a signal for damaged goods to be brought out at once. All our meat turned out to be tough. There was hardly any crust to our bread. We seemed to pay enough to keep the basement filled with food. And the worst fact of all was that we never had any food in the house!

One of our messes was a little dinner for Traddles. I had met him in town and asked him to walk home with me that evening. He agreed, and I wrote to Dora that he was coming for dinner. It was pleasant weather, and we had a fine walk.

The dinner was a different matter altogether. I could not have wished for a prettier wife at the table. I could have wished for more room. Poor Traddles was so hemmed in that I wondered if he could use his knife and fork.

There was another thing I could have wished— that Jip not walk on the dinner table. Putting his foot in the melted butter added a little something more to the mess.

I could also have wished for a better meal. The oysters that Dora bought could not be opened because we had no knives. The meat was barely cooked. But by luck we had some bacon in the kitchen. We ate that.

At least my writing was going well. I sold many of my pieces to magazines. Even better, I was writing my first book.

I was deep in thought about my book when I passed Mrs. Steerforth's house one evening. The

maid met me and asked me to come in and talk to Miss Dartle. Rosa Dartle was a young woman who took care of Steerforth's mother. I went in to see her.

"I am told you wish to speak to me, Miss Dartle," I said.

"If you please," she said. "Has Emily been found?"

I had heard nothing about little Emily and my friend since they left together. I said so to Miss Dartle.

"She has run away!"

"Run away?" I repeated.

"Yes! From him," she said. "If she is not found, perhaps she will never be found. She may be dead!"

She then surprised me by calling Littimer, Steerforth's servant, into the room. He told a chilling story.

Steerforth and little Emily had been all over Europe since they left Yarmouth. Little Emily was greatly admired wherever they went. However, she was often in low spirits. She and Steerforth argued a lot and he finally left her. At that, little Emily tried to kill herself. Littimer had tried to watch over her, but she got away from him.

"She got out a window that I had nailed up myself," said Littimer. "She climbed down a vine and has not been seen or heard from since."

The next evening I went to see Mr. Peggotty to tell him what I had learned from Littimer. I found him reading by a window. The room was neat and orderly. I saw in a moment that it had been kept prepared for Emily's return.

Mr. Peggotty listened quietly as I told him the story. When I had finished, he shaded his face and remained silent for a long while. Finally he said, "My niece, Emily, is alive, sir! I know she's alive!"

Before I left that night Mr. Peggotty prepared Emily's room for what he hoped would be her return home. Carefully, he arranged a candle and a dress to be waiting for Emily. I left without appearing to notice his sad gesture.

Meanwhile, I continued to work hard on my book without letting my other duties slip. When it finally came out, the book was very successful. I did not let the praise go to my head. I did, however, give up my magazine work.

I had then been married about a year and a half. Dora and I had tried a number of servants, none of whom lasted. We finally gave up housekeeping. The house kept itself. Instead we hired a page to run our errands. It turned out that his main job was to quarrel with the cook.

Sad to say, he also stole from us. He took Dora's watch, which, like everything else we owned, was kept in no particular place. When the police caught the page we learned even more. He had taken wine from the cellar and food from the kitchen and had given coals to the milkman. Something had to be done about the management of our house. I told Dora how I felt, but she did not listen.

I then decided to "form her mind," as the saying goes. I talked to her about subjects that were on my mind. I read Shakespeare to her. I tried to give her little bits of useful information. I found myself being a schoolteacher to her, but nothing helped. It became clear to me that Dora's mind was already formed.

Sometimes I would wonder, "What might have happened if Dora and I had never known each other?" I sometimes thought about the dreams and happy days with Agnes in my youth.

I always loved Dora, so I made up my mind to stop trying to change her. She was truly fond of me and proud of me. I let it go at that.

Dora and I were filled with joy when the doctor told us that she was going to have a baby. Quickly, though, the joy faded. Dora was not very strong, and the baby died shortly after birth. Almost at once, Dora's health got worse.

I began to carry her down the stairs every morning and up the stairs every night. As the days passed, she grew lighter in my arms. I tried not to think about this much, but one night it hit me especially hard. My aunt left Dora with the parting "Good night, little blossom." At that I sat down alone at my desk and cried. Oh, what a fatal name it was. How the blossom wilts in its bloom upon the tree!

9 Comings and Goings

One morning I received at the office a long and flowery letter from Mr. Micawber. It is hard to describe the letter. It was filled with words and sentences that made very little sense. Mr. Micawber seemed to be trying to say something important. Yet his meaning was well hidden. I could make out that he wanted to meet Traddles and me at the King's Bench Prison. What for, I could not tell.

As I was reading the letter the third time, Tommy Traddles walked into my office. I asked him to read the letter, which he did. He was as much in the dark as I. Tommy said that Mr. Micawber had started working at the office of Wickfield and Heep. He didn't know anything else about it.

We agreed to meet Micawber, as he had asked. Although we were a quarter of an hour early, Mr. Micawber was waiting for us. "Gentlemen!" he said, "You are friends in need and friends indeed."

We greeted him warmly, as old friends do. We followed that with a good deal of talk about things in general. Then, after a brief silence, I asked, "How is our friend Heep?"

"My dear Copperfield," Mr. Micawber replied.

"I do not wish to talk about him." He turned pale as he spoke. Then he got quite excited.

I apologized for touching on a subject that upset him. "May I ask how Mr. and Miss Wickfield are?" I added.

"Miss Wickfield is, as always, a bright light. My dear Copperfield, she is a star in this miserable life." Having said that, he broke down and cried.

Traddles and I were at a loss as to what to say next. I finally got the idea to invite him to my aunt's house. I thought we could talk better there. Traddles urged him to agree.

"Gentlemen, do with me as you will," he replied. "I am a straw upon the surface of the ocean. I am tossed in all directions by the elephants. I beg your pardon—I should have said the elements."

We went to my aunt's house rather than to mine because of Dora's ill health. After being sent for, my aunt greeted us and welcomed Mr. Micawber. He kissed her hand and took a seat by the window.

After a while, my aunt said, "I hope Mrs. Micawber and your family are well, sir."

Mr. Micawber bowed his head. "They are as well, ma'am, as servants can ever hope to be."

"Lord bless you, sir," said my aunt. "What are you talking about?"

Mr. Micawber finally let us know what had him so upset. It was the man he worked for, Uriah Heep. He called Heep a snake and a cheat and a liar. He vowed that he would crush him. "I will lead this life no longer!" he yelled.

I never saw a man so upset in my life. The longer he spoke, the hotter he got. I had some fear of his dying on the spot. Suddenly, though, he rushed out of the house. His last words called for a meeting the following week, at which he would tell us everything about Heep. Then he was gone.

By this time, some months had passed since we had heard about Emily and Steerforth. I felt that Emily was dead, but Mr. Peggotty did not give up hope. He was sure she was alive somewhere. We were soon to learn that he was right. Not only was she alive, but also she came back to us. The story of her return is as follows.

In order to escape from Steerforth, Emily ran off during the night. She ran along the beach until she was too tired to go on. Then she fell asleep. When she awoke, a woman whom she knew was standing over her. The woman took her home, cared for her, and arranged for her to go to France by boat.

Emily got to France and took a job waiting on ladies at an inn. One day Steerforth or Littimer appeared. (Emily said "that snake," so we weren't sure which one it was. We never did find out for sure, but I believe it was Steerforth.) In any case, the "snake" did not see her. She packed her things at once and left for England.

She longed to go straight to Yarmouth, but she could not. Fear that her uncle hated her and fear that people would point at her kept her away. She went instead to London. It was there that a good friend found her and brought her home to Mr. Peggotty.

Upon her return, Mr. Peggotty was quick to tell me, "Our future lies over the sea, Master Davy. No one can bother my darling in Australia. We will begin a new life there."

I asked if he knew when they could leave.

"There will be a ship sailing in about six weeks. We'll be on it," he said.

"Just you and Emily?" I asked.

"Yes, Master Davy. My sister is too fond of you and yours to go."

"Poor Ham!" I said.

"My good sister takes care of his house," said Mr. Peggotty. "They sit and talk together," he added.

The very next day Mr. Peggotty locked the door on his old houseboat for the last time. He and Emily took a coach to London. They planned to stay there until their ship sailed for Australia.

Now I must get back to the story of Mr. Micawber. It is, as you will see, connected with the story of Mr. Peggotty.

I had last seen Mr. Micawber at Aunt Betsey's house, where he requested a mysterious meeting to expose Uriah Heep. Now, a week later, Aunt Betsey and Traddles and I were called together so that Micawber could reveal this true "snake" to us. Though she was ill, Dora insisted she could manage without us while we went to the meeting.

We accompanied Micawber to the office of Wickfield and Heep, which was located in Mr. Wickfield's house. We were led into Mr. Wickfield's former office. There we were surprised to find Uriah Heep in place of Wickfield. Mr. Wickfield was again sick in bed.

Uriah Heep, assuming that we had come to see him or Agnes, turned to dismiss Mr. Micawber, as he was used to doing.

"Don't wait, Micawber," said Uriah.

Mr. Micawber did not move.

"What are you waiting for?" said Uriah. "Micawber, did you hear me tell you not to wait?"

"Yes!" answered Mr. Micawber.

"Then why do you wait?"

"Because I choose to."

Uriah's face lost color. "You are a scoundrel, as all the world knows. Go along! I'll talk to you shortly."

"If there is a scoundrel on this earth, it is you," said Mr. Micawber.

Uriah fell back, as if he had been struck or stung.

Then the charges against Uriah Heep burst from Mr. Micawber's mouth. Heep's crimes were laid out, one after another: He had stolen money from Mr. Wickfield. He had forged Mr. Wickfield's name to papers that gave him power over the Wickfield family. He planned to take over the Wickfield business. Mr. Micawber was able to prove each of these charges.

When he had finished, and Uriah Heep was destroyed, Mr. Micawber was finally at peace. "The cloud is passed from my mind," he said. "Nothing will ever bother me again!"

My dear aunt, who was always looking to help others, then came up with a wonderful idea. Would Mr. Micawber like to get a fresh start in Australia? Would he like to go there with Mr. Peggotty and Emily? Would he accept a loan so that he and his family could make the trip? Yes! Yes! Yes! Mr. Micawber was as happy as I'd ever seen him.

As I walked him back to his hotel, Mr. Micawber seemed as though he had already left England. Already he was looking at the passing cows with the eye of an Australian farmer.

10 Darkness Before My Eyes

The matter of the stolen money was settled quite effectively by Traddles. My old school friend acted as Mr. Micawber's lawyer and cleared Micawber of all suspicion with regard to the stolen money. Then he got a large sum of the money back from Heep. He also forced the villain to give up all claims to Mr. Wickfield's business, which was not worth much.

Following the meeting with Uriah Heep, I accompanied my aunt to her house. She and I sat alone, as we used to, before going to bed. She said, "Trot, I have something on my mind. Do you wish to know?"

"Indeed, I do, Aunt. If you have sorrow, I should like to share it."

"You have sorrow enough, child," said my aunt, warmly.

"Please tell me now," I said.

"Would you ride with me a little way tomorrow morning?" asked my aunt.

"Of course."

"At nine," she said. "I'll tell you then, my dear."

At nine the next morning we went out in a carriage and drove to London. We drove a long way through the streets until we came to a large hospital. Standing by the hospital was a hearse. My aunt waved to the driver, and he drove off. We followed.

"Trot, that was my husband. We have been separated for many years. He was a gambler and a cheat. I didn't want anyone to know."

"Did he die in the hospital?"

"Yes."

She sat quietly beside me. A tear ran down her face.

"He was there once before," she said. "He was sick a long time. When he knew his condition this last time, he asked them to send for me. He was sorry then. Very sorry."

"You went, I know, Aunt."

"I went. I was with him a good deal afterward."

We drove away, out of town, to the churchyard at Hornsey. "Better here than in the streets," said my aunt. "He was born here."

We got out and followed the coffin to a corner, where the service was read.

"Six and thirty years ago this day I was married," said my aunt as we walked back to the carriage. "God forgive us all."

We took our seats in silence. She sat beside me, holding my hand for a long time. Eventually she burst into tears. "He was a fine man when I married him, Trot. He was sadly changed."

I soon returned home to Dora, whose health did not improve. I do not know how long she was ill. It was not long in weeks or months, but it was a weary, weary while. I began to fear that I would never again see my wife running with her old friend Jip. Poor Jip had grown very old. His sight had become weak; and his limbs, feeble. It may be only that he missed Dora. For whatever reason, he now spent all of his time lying at the side of her bed.

One evening I was sitting beside Dora on her bed. We were silent for a few moments, and then she turned to me.

"Davy."

"My dear Dora!"

"I know Mr. Wickfield is not well, but I very much want to see Agnes."

"I will write to her, my dear."

"Do you think she will come?"

"I am certain of it. I have only to ask her, and she is sure to come."

"Give Agnes my dear love and tell her that I want very, very much to see her. I have nothing left to wish for."

"Except to get well again, Dora."

"Oh, Davy! Sometimes I think that that will never be."

Agnes came at once. On the day she arrived, we sat together all day with Dora, who was quite

cheerful. However, when Dora and I were alone that night Dora's mood changed.

"Davy, I am going to say something that I have often thought of saying. You won't mind, will you?"

"Of course I won't mind, my darling," I said.

"Davy dear, I am afraid that I was too young. I don't mean in years only. I mean in experience and thoughts and everything. I have begun to think I was not fit to be a wife."

I tried to stop my tears, but I could not. "Oh, Dora, you are as fit to be a wife as I am to be a husband," I cried. Then I added, "We have been very happy."

"Don't cry, then," she said. "I want to speak to Agnes alone. Please send her up to me."

I went down and gave Agnes the message. She disappeared, leaving me alone with Jip. I sat down by the fire. Jip looked at me and walked to the door. He whined to go up to Dora.

"Not tonight, Jip! Not tonight!"

He came back to me very slowly, licked my hands, and lifted his dim eyes to my face.

"Oh, Jip! It may be, never again!"

He lay down at my feet, stretched himself out as if to sleep, and died.

"Oh, Agnes! Look, look here!"

She was coming down the stairs. Her face was full of pity and sorrow.

"Agnes?"

It was over. Darkness came before my eyes, and for a time things were blotted out.

When I awoke from my collapse, Agnes was with me, giving me words of hope and peace. She was like a holy being in my house. I thought again how much she was like a stained glass window in the church. Her gentle face, like one from heaven, softened my pain.

I felt that the future was closed to me now that Dora was gone. I could know no peace but in the grave. Yet Agnes knew better. Dear, sweet, kind Agnes decided what was best for me. I was to travel outside England. The change would bring back peace to my mind, she said.

Still, I could not leave at once. I had to wait to bid farewell to the group leaving for Australia.

11 I Leave England

I now must tell about an awful event in my life. For years after it happened, I dreamed of it often. I still wake up at night in the quiet of my room disturbed by it. As plainly as I can see it, I will try to write down what happened.

The time was drawing near for the sailing of the ship to Australia. My good old nurse, Peggotty, came up to London. I spent all of my time with her and her brother and the Micawbers. I never saw Emily.

One night I remembered that Ham had asked me to write a note to Emily for him. He wanted her to know that he was not mad at her for running off with Steerforth. Indeed, he wanted her to know that he blamed himself. He knew he should not have tried to marry her and make her stay in a fishing village. I decided to write the note to her before she left the country. She might want me to deliver some parting words to Ham.

I sat down in my room and wrote to her. I left the note out, to be sent in the morning.

The next day I slept late. I was awakened by my aunt at my bedside.

"Trot, my dear," she said as I opened my eyes.

"Mr. Peggotty is here. Shall he come up?"

I said yes, and he soon appeared.

As we shook hands, he told me, "Master Davy, I gave Emily your note. She wrote a letter back to Ham. Will you please read it? If you see no harm in it, Emily asks that you get it to Ham."

I opened it and read as follows:

> I have got your message. Oh, what can I write to thank you for your kindness to me! I have put your words close to my heart. I shall keep them till I die. Good-bye my dear friend. All thanks and blessings. Farewell evermore.

"May I tell her you'll take charge of it, Master Davy?" said Mr. Peggotty.

"Yes, of course," I said. "I'll take it down to Yarmouth myself. There's time for me to go and come back before the ship sails. I'll go down tonight."

I got the box seat on the mail coach to Yarmouth. As we left London, I said something to the driver about the strange color of the sky.

"That's wind, sir," he said. "There will be trouble at sea before long."

There was a wind all day. As night drew near, dark clouds rolled in, and the wind blew harder and harder. Sheets of rain forced us to stop whenever we found a tree, in order to protect the horses.

When morning came, it blew harder still. We struggled on. When we came within sight of the sea, the waves looked like tall buildings. As we got into Yarmouth, the people came outside to greet us. They could hardly believe that the mail had come through such a night.

I took a room at the old inn and then went down to look at the sea. On the beach, I found desperate, wailing women, whose husbands were away in boats. Old sailors were among the people staring at the rough and dangerous enemy.

I did not find Ham in this crowd, so I went back to the inn and to bed. I was shortly awakened, however, by a knocking on the door. The storm was still raging.

"What is the matter?" I cried.

"A wreck! Close by!"

I jumped out of bed and ran to the water's edge. I saw the ship close to shore. One mast was broken off, and she lay over on her side. As I watched, a great wave rolled over the wreck. It washed men and parts of the ship into the raging sea. It was an awful sight.

People were screaming, the storm was roaring, and the dying ship was groaning. And then, to my horror, I saw Ham. He was trying to reach the

remaining sailors on the ship. He had a rope tied around his waist, and he was swimming out to the wreck. But he never made it. The ship broke apart before he got to it. He was close enough, though, that pieces of the sinking ship struck him. Men on the shore finally pulled his rope in. They pulled him in to my very feet. Ham was dead, beaten to death by the raging sea. The men carried his body to the nearest house. As I sat beside his bed, a man who had known me when I was a child called my name.

"Sir, will you come out? A body has come ashore," he said, as he led me to the shore.

"Do I know it?" I asked.

He answered nothing. On that part of the shore where Emily and I had looked for shells, I saw him lying. His head was upon his arm, as I had often seen him lie at school. It was Steerforth.

The shock of watching Ham die and then of seeing Steerforth's body was almost more than I could bear. The pain was added to that which I had recently suffered in the death of Dora.

I returned home a wrecked man.

At once I decided to hide what had happened from Mr. Peggotty and Emily. I took Mr. Micawber aside that same night to ask his help. He promised to keep all newspapers from Mr. Peggotty. He was true to his word.

Sailing day came. All of those who were leaving

except Mr. Micawber remained unaware of the deaths of Ham and Steerforth.

We parted on the deck of the ship. I hugged Mr. Peggotty and then took his weeping sister away with me. Peggotty and I climbed over the side of their ship and into our own small boat. We sat at a little distance and watched the ship go off on her course. Emily was at her uncle's side. She and Mr. Peggotty were standing high on the deck. As they passed on, she was clinging to him, and he was holding her. Seeing us, Emily waved her last goodbye to me.

For me the night was a long and gloomy one. The ghosts of many hopes and many sorrows bothered me.

Shortly thereafter, I left England and all who were dear to me. I did not know, even then, how great the grief was inside of me. I cried for my first love and for my child wife. I mourned a boyhood friend; and I mourned the broken heart that had found rest in the stormy sea. I longed for the simple home where I had heard the night wind blowing when I was a child.

For many months I traveled. I was in Switzerland when a letter from Agnes reached me. She was happy. The school she had opened to support her father was doing well. That was all she told me about herself. She also said that she knew I would turn things around for myself. She knew that sorrow would make me strong rather than weak. She was proud of what I had done but prouder yet of what I was still to do.

Her words lifted my spirits. I was not ready to go home at once, but I was more at peace with myself. I carried her letter with me everywhere.

Soon I returned to my writing. The more I wrote, the more I became my old self. Finally, after three years of travel, I returned to England. Home was very dear to me—and Agnes, too.

12 My One True Love

I landed in London on a winter evening. It was dark and raining. I saw more fog and mud in a minute than I had seen in a year.

In my letters, I had written that I would be home around Christmas time. I came earlier, though, so I might have the pleasure of taking everyone by surprise.

I went first to see Traddles. He had an apartment on Holborn Court.

"Good God!" cried Traddles, as he met me at the door. "It's Copperfield!" He rushed into my arms, where I held him tight.

"All well, my dear Traddles."

"All well, my dear, dear Copperfield. And nothing but good news, I hope!"

We cried with pleasure, both of us.

"My dear fellow," said Traddles, "how glad I am to see you."

I was so filled with joy that I was unable to speak.

"My dear fellow!" he said again. "And grown so famous!" (I had written another book, which was selling well.) "When did you come? Where have you come from? What have you been doing?"

He never stopped for an answer to anything although he had many questions. He hugged me again, and I hugged him. We were both laughing and wiping our eyes as we sat down.

"To think that you were so close to home and not at the ceremony," he said.

"What ceremony, my dear Traddles?"

"Didn't you get my letter? Why, my dear Copperfield, I am married!"

"Married!" I cried joyfully.

"Lord bless me, yes!" said Traddles. "Here is Sophy now."

Mrs. Traddles came into the room. She was a cheerful, happy, bright-looking bride. I kissed her and told her how happy I was for her and Traddles.

We sat and talked for a long while. I learned that Traddles was doing well in his law work and that the future looked bright for them.

Mrs. Traddles made tea and toast, which we enjoyed very much. She had seen Agnes, she told me, on a wedding trip to Kent. She had seen my aunt there, too. Both my aunt and Agnes were well, and they had talked of nothing but me.

It was very late when I wished Traddles and Sophy goodnight. I walked back to Gray's Inn, where I was staying. My eyes fell upon the face of a man I had not seen in many years. It was Mr. Chillip, the doctor who helped bring me into the world.

I walked up to where he was sitting and said, "How do you do, Mr. Chillip?"

He was greatly flustered by this greeting from a stranger.

"You don't remember me?" I asked.

"Well, sir, I kind of do, but I couldn't lay my hand on your name," he said. I wasn't surprised. He hadn't seen me for more than ten years. On hearing my name, he was very moved.

"In what part of the country do you live now?" I asked, seating myself near him.

"I live within a few miles of Bury St. Edmund's," said Mr. Chillip. "Your stepfather is again a neighbor of mine."

"I heard that Mr. Murdstone had married again," I said.

"Married a young lady with a lot of money, poor thing."

"How is the present Mrs. Murdstone?" I asked.

"Mrs. Chillip's opinion is that her spirit has been broken since her marriage. Mrs. Chillip thinks she has gone mad."

"And Miss Murdstone?" I said.

"She lives with her brother and his wife. They are not liked very much."

I told him that I was going down to my aunt's early in the morning. I told him that she was one of the most tenderhearted of women. He remembered the night of my birth and trembled at the thought of ever seeing her again.

"Is that so indeed, sir? Really?" he said. Then he called for a candle and excused himself for the evening.

Every bone in my body was tired, so I, too, went to bed.

The next day I took the coach to Dover and burst into my aunt's house while she was having tea. Dear old Peggotty, who acted as housekeeper, was there. We greeted each other with open arms and tears.

My aunt and I talked far into the night. She told me of the cheerful and hopeful letters from Australia. "And when, Trot, are you going over to Canterbury?" she asked.

"Tomorrow morning," I said.

"You will find Mr. Wickfield a white-haired old man. But in all other respects, he is a better man."

"What about Agnes?" I asked.

"You will find her as good and as beautiful as ever. If I knew higher praise, Trot, I would give it to her."

There was no praise high enough for Agnes. Oh, why had I gone so far away!

"Has she any . . . any sweetheart?"

"She could have married many times," my aunt said. "But, Trot, she seems to have a special devotion."

"Well, Agnes will tell me at her own good time," I said.

We sat, looking into the past, without saying another word until we parted for the night.

I rode away early in the morning for the scene of my old school days. I was not quite happy even though I would soon look upon her face again.

I went on foot to the old house. Inside I passed the room where first Uriah Heep and later Mr. Micawber had worked. I saw now that there was no office. Otherwise, the house was just as I first saw it.

The opening of the little door in the wall made me jump and turn. Her beautiful eyes met mine as she came toward me. She stopped and started to fall. I caught her in my arms. "Agnes, my dear girl! I have come too suddenly upon you."

"No, no! I am so happy to see you, Trotwood!"

"Dear Agnes, the happiness is mine to see you once again."

I wanted to tell her how good she was and how much I owed her and how dear she was to me. But I could not say the words.

"Tell me of yourself, Agnes. How are you?"

"Papa is well. Our home is as it used to be. I am busy at my school. There's really not much to tell."

We talked and talked. When it was time for me to leave, she put her hand in mine and said that she was proud of me.

I must interrupt my tale here to say one more word about Traddles. He received a letter from Mr. Creakle, he who beat us with canes at old Salem House. Mr. Creakle now ran what was said to be a model prison. Any prisoner who did something wrong was put in a cell by himself and allowed no contact with others. It was said that this was a sure way to make prisoners behave.

Mr. Creakle asked Traddles to visit his prison. Traddles asked me to go with him. So we went and looked. We were only mildly impressed until we came upon the cells of prisoners number twenty-seven and number twenty-eight. Can you believe it? Number twenty-seven was Uriah Heep, who was in for signing other people's names to checks. Number twenty-eight was Littimer, who had tried to rob his new master. It was an odd thing to see how things could change.

When the year came round to Christmastime, I had been home about two months. I had seen Agnes a lot. I rode to see her at least once a week.

One very fateful day my aunt put her head out the door and said, "Riding today, Trot?"

"Yes," I said. "I am going over to Canterbury. It's a good day for a ride."

"I hope your horse may think so," said my aunt. "At present, he looks as if he'd rather be in his stable."

My aunt, I should say, allowed my horse on the lawn. She had not at all changed her rule against donkeys.

"Trot."

"Yes?"

"I think Agnes is going to be married."

It was a short ride to Canterbury that day. I found her alone by the fire, reading. She welcomed me as she always did. We spoke of the things that had happened since we were children. Finally, I had to tell her.

"When I loved Dora . . ."

"Yes!" she cried.

"When I loved her, my love would not have been complete without your kind support. When I lost her, Agnes, I would have been nothing without you."

Her sweet eyes were shining through her tears.

"I went away, dear Agnes, loving you. I stayed away loving you. I returned home loving you."

And then I asked her to marry me.

"I am so blessed, Trotwood. My heart is overjoyed. But there is one thing I must say."

"What, dear?"

She laid her gentle hands on my shoulders and looked calmly into my face.

"Do you know yet what it is?"

"I am afraid to guess. Tell me, my dear."

"I have loved you all my life."

We were married within two weeks. It was a quiet

wedding, with only Traddles and Sophy as guests. Full of joy we left them and drove away together.

"Dearest husband!" said Agnes. "Now that I may call you by that name, I have one thing more to tell you."

"Let me hear it, love."

"It is from the night when Dora died. She sent you for me."

"She did."

"She told me that she wished to leave me something. Can you imagine what it was?"

I drew the wife who had loved me so long closer to my side. I thought that I could.

Agnes went on, "She told me that she wished to make a last request."

"And it was?"

"That only I would occupy this vacant place."

Agnes laid her head upon my shoulder and wept. I wept with her then though we were very happy. Such is the ending of my story.

Epilogue

What I have set out to record is nearly finished. Yet my story would be incomplete if I did not tell you about a visitor who came to see Agnes and me.

I had been married ten happy years. I had also gained fame and fortune as a writer. Then one night in spring Agnes and I were sitting by the fire together. Three of our children were playing in the room. By and by I was told that a stranger wished to see me.

My servant had asked the man if he had come on business. The stranger had answered no. He had come for the pleasure of seeing me—and he had come a long way. He was an old man, my servant said, and looked like a farmer.

To the children, this sounded very mysterious, like the beginning of a fairy tale. One of our boys laid his head on his mother's lap to be out of harm's way. Little Agnes, our oldest child, peeked from between the window curtains to see what would happen next.

"Let him come in here," I said.

There soon appeared a hardy, gray-haired old man. Attracted by his looks, little Agnes ran to bring him in. I had not yet clearly seen his face when my wife cried out that it was Mr. Peggotty.

It was indeed Mr. Peggotty. He was an old man now but still healthy and strong in his old age. Once we had finished our first glad greetings, I looked at him carefully. With the fire shining on his face, he looked as handsome an old man as I had ever seen.

"Master Davy," he said. "It's a joyful thing to see you and your own true wife."

"A joyful hour indeed, old friend!" I cried.

"Are you alone?" asked Agnes.

"Yes, ma'am," he said, kissing her hand. "Quite alone."

We sat him between us, not knowing how to give him enough welcome. As I listened to him talk, I could hear no change in his way of speaking.

"It's a lot of water to come across and only stay for four weeks," Mr. Peggoty was saying. "But water comes natural to me. And friends are dear, and I am here."

"Are you going back those many thousand miles so soon?" asked Agnes.

"Yes, ma'am," he said. "I gave the promise to Emily before I left. You see, I don't grow younger as the years pass. If I hadn't sailed when I did, most likely I never would have done it. It's always been on my mind that I must come and see Master Davy and you before I get to be too old."

He looked at us as if he could never see enough of us. Agnes laughingly pushed back some locks of his gray hair so that he might see us better.

"How are you doing?" I asked.

"We are as well to do as well could be. What with raising sheep and cows and one thing and another, we're getting by," said Mr. Peggotty.

"And Emily?" asked Agnes and I, together.

"Emily is doing fine," he said, "She and I heard the terrible news about Ham a year or so after it happened."

"Did it change her much?" we asked.

"Yes, for a good long time," he said. "You wouldn't know her now, though. She has soft, sorrowful blue eyes. She has a delicate face and a quiet voice. She could have married several times but didn't. She likes to teach children and to tend to sick people. She's always cheerful and loving with me. That's Emily!"

"And what is the news of Mr. Micawber?" I asked. "We know he has paid off all his bills here. He must be doing well."

"Indeed he is," said Mr. Peggotty. "I never wish to meet a better gentleman. He has an important government job. Everybody likes and admires him."

We talked much of Mr. Micawber on many other evenings while Mr. Peggotty stayed with us. He lived with us during the whole term of his stay, which was something less than a month. His sister and my aunt came to London to see him. Agnes and I said good-bye to him aboard ship when he sailed. We shall never part from him again.

Before he left, Mr. Peggotty went with me to Yarmouth. He wanted to see a little stone tablet I had put in the churchyard in memory of Ham. As I was copying the inscription for him, he bent down and got a piece of grass and a little dirt from the grave.

"For Emily," he said. "I promised her, Master Davy."

And now my written story ends. I look back once more before I close these pages.

I see myself, with Agnes at my side, moving along the road of life. I see our children and our friends around us. I hear the roar of many voices. Whose faces are the clearest to me? Aunt Betsey's and Peggotty's.

Here is my aunt in stronger eyeglasses—now an old woman of 80 years and more, She walks several miles a day, even in bad weather. My aunt's old disappointment is set right, now. She is godmother to a real living Betsey Trotwood, whom Dora, our next oldest, says she spoils.

Always with my aunt is Peggotty, my good old nurse. Her cheeks and arms are wrinkled. Her eyes that used to shine so brightly are fainter now. She carries an old, worn-out book in her pocket and shows it lovingly to the children. It is the one from which I read to her when I was a child.

I am also reminded of the face of my dear old Traddles. He is busy in his office. His hair is made wild by the constant rubbing of his lawyer's wig. His desk is covered with thick piles of paper. He will be a judge one day—and a good one. We walk along together, arm in arm, to a family dinner.

And now as I close my story, these faces fade away. But one face is above them and beyond them all. I turn my head and see it beside me. My lamp burns low, and I have written far into the night. But the dear person, without whom I would be nothing, keeps me company.

Oh, Agnes. Oh, my soul. May your face be by me when I close my life. May I still find you near, pointing upward!